"Here is a loving, tender-hearted, gospel-confident pastor, calling pastors to be loving, tender-hearted, gospel-confident counselors. David Powlison lived the message of this book and gave his life to mobilizing the church to believe it and live it as well. If you're a pastor, this book is a must-read, but not just once. Read it again and again, praying that its beautiful vision would become your daily ministry model."

Paul David Tripp, President, Paul Tripp Ministries; author, *New Morning Mercies* and *My Heart Cries Out*

"It is a rare privilege to get to hear from someone who devoted his life to being good at one thing. That is what you hold—a conversation with David Powlison about what it means to be a pastor who counsels well. That is what David devoted his life to exploring. Learn from him about the beauty and unique opportunities that emerge from counseling as a pastor, and every area of your ministry (teaching, preaching, mentoring, administration) will be enriched. Your ability to serve as an ambassador of Christ to those who are hurting will be enhanced."

Brad Hambrick, Pastor of Counseling, The Summit Church, Durham, North Carolina

"David Powlison was a remarkable man. Out of his passion that the church of Jesus Christ take up the mantle of care for broken human beings in this fallen world, he became the quintessential leader of the biblical counseling movement. Out of his incredible gifting to communicate this with beauty and grace, he became one of the most compelling Christian authors of his generation. As a busy pastor myself, I promise that you and your church need to hear what Powlison has to say. If you are looking for a glorious, compelling, and clear introduction to the heart of Christ for his church, you will not find a better place to start than this book."

Heath Lambert, Senior Pastor, First Baptist Church of Jacksonville; Executive Director, Association of Certified Biblical Counselors; author, *A Theology of Biblical Counseling* and *Finally Free*

"David Powlison's book is a profoundly fitting final gift to the church. It is a book that takes us to the very heart of everything David believed the church and her pastors should be, a vision that is simultaneously thrilling and challenging, visionary and practical, theologically rich and culturally astute. My work as a pastor is so much better because of it. This book will expand your pastoral ambitions and encourage you to be more like Christ. Every pastor will profit from it."

Steve Midgley, Executive Director, Biblical Counselling UK; Senior Minister, Christ Church Cambridge; coauthor, *The Heart of Anger*

"Pastors have unique opportunities to counsel unlike anyone else. With his typically rich insights and thought-provoking analysis, David Powlison encourages pastors to counsel and shepherd their church members. Buy a copy and give this Christ-honoring book to your pastor. He'll be strengthened and encouraged through it!"

Deepak Reju, Pastor of Biblical Counseling and Family Ministry, Capitol Hill Baptist Church, Washington, DC; author, *The Pastor and Counseling*

"When our preaching reaches people's hearts with the gospel, it raises as many questions as it answers. That's where our pastoral counseling comes in—gentle, honest conversations with sinners and sufferers who want Jesus at their personal point of need. David Powlison is a faithful guide, helping us pastors fulfill this deeper ministry, where people get traction for newness of life."

Ray Ortlund, President, Renewal Ministries

The Pastor as Counselor

Other Crossway books by David Powlison

God's Grace in Your Suffering (2018)

How Does Sanctification Work? (2017)

Making All Things New: Restoring Joy to the Sexually Broken (2017)

The Pastor as Counselor

The Call for Soul Care

David Powlison

Foreword by Ed Welch

WHEATON, ILLINOIS

Cover design and image: Crystal Courtney

First printing 2021

Printed in the United States of America

Unless otherwise indicated, Scripture quotations are from the ESV® Bible (The Holy Bible, English Standard Version®), copyright © 2001 by Crossway, a publishing ministry of Good News Publishers. Used by permission. All rights reserved.

Trade paperback ISBN: 978-1-4335-7301-9
ePub ISBN: 978-1-4335-7304-0
PDF ISBN: 978-1-4335-7302-6
Mobipocket ISBN: 978-1-4335-7303-3

Library of Congress Cataloging-in-Publication Data

Names: Powlison, David, 1949-2019 author.
Title: The pastor as counselor : the call for soul care / David Powlison.
Description: Wheaton, Illinois : Crossway, 2021. | Includes bibliographical references and index.
Identifiers: LCCN 2020035588 (print) | LCCN 2020035589 (ebook) | ISBN 9781433573019 (trade paperback) | ISBN 9781433573033 (mobipocket) | ISBN 9781433573026 (pdf)
Subjects: LCSH: Pastoral counseling. | Pastoral care. | Counseling—Religious aspects—Christianity.
Classification: LCC BV4012.2 .P658 2021 (print) | LCC BV4012.2 (ebook) | DDC 253.5—dc23
LC record available at https://lccn.loc.gov/2020035588
LC ebook record available at https://lccn.loc.gov/2020035589

Crossway is a publishing ministry of Good News Publishers.

LB		30	29	28	27	26	25	24	23	22	21
15	14	13	12	11	10	9	8	7	6	5	4	3	2	1

Contents

Foreword

I AM SO PLEASED TO INTRODUCE this concise monograph from David Powlison. As with most of David's writings, this is a rich banquet. You will return to it and find more. I am also sad that this is a posthumous publication. David went to be with the one he loved above all others in June 2019. Reading *The Pastor as Counselor*, I miss him all the more.

David was a polymath who knew much about many things. After working with him for almost forty years I still chuckled at his passing references to specific flowers, trees, and birds; quotes from early church fathers; details of a solar event scheduled to appear later that evening; and trivia about Philadelphia sports—those references made all the more amazing because he grew up in Hawaii and spent his pre-CCEF (Christian Counseling & Educational Foundation) years in Boston. But these were peripheral adornments on a man who knew Jesus and loved him, fed on the word, was wholly engaged with the person in front of him, and could enjoy teasing close friends and family (and was happy to be teased). He went through life knowing that he was created in God's image yet also had much in common with the grass of the field that passes quickly. All this might not be enough of an introduction to persuade you to love him as I and many others do, but perhaps it is enough for you to know that he will be a trustworthy and engaging guide to the pastor as counselor

For all its practical direction, this book is not intended to be a how-to manual. It is more a marker that clarifies your place in this sometimes confusing world of counseling. It reminds you that—right now—you have much counsel you *can* offer to others and already *have* offered, and imagines the path ahead. It will serve you both as an introduction to biblical counseling and as a long-term mentor.

David will persuade you that your ministry is both the public ministry and private ministry of the word. Pastoral care includes both. He will keep larger culture matters in view, especially the psychotherapies and their reputations to go deep and cure souls. In contrast he lets Scripture state what we all know: God alone reveals the depths of the heart and its cure in the gospel of Jesus Christ. We might not be the most skilled practitioners. Yet Scripture accents how weak, prayerful, and loving friends are the pastoral engine of our churches. It also leads us in always-growing wisdom in "the art of arts," which is Gregory the Great's description of pastoral care and counsel.

David's questions throughout this volume will cause you to assess where you are in your own counseling theory and skills. Like all good questions, each could provoke fruitful reflection and stimulating conversations with colleagues and friends. All this will make *The Pastor as Counselor* the thickest small book you have ever studied. My fifth read was as helpful as the first.

Edward T. Welch

Introduction

PASTOR, YOU *ARE* A COUNSELOR.

Perhaps you don't think of yourself that way. Perhaps you don't want to be a counselor. But you are one.

Perhaps preaching, leadership, and administration keep you preoccupied, and you do not do much hands-on pastoral work. You don't take time for serious talking with people. In effect, you are counseling your people to think that most of us don't need the give-and-take of candid, constructive conversation. Apparently, the care and cure of wayward, distractible, battered, immature souls—people like us—can be handled by public ministry and private devotion. The explicit wisdom of both Scripture and church history argues to the contrary.

Perhaps you are a poor counselor. Are you shy, tentative, passive? Are you aggressive, controlling, opinionated? Do you sympathize with strugglers so much that you have trouble shifting the conversation into forward gear? Do people feel you don't listen well and don't really care, so they don't find reasons to trust you?

Unlike Proverbs, do you moralize, unhinging advice from deeper insight and deeper reasons? "Read your Bible. . . . Just get accountable. . . . Have your quiet time. . . . Get involved in a ministry."

Unlike the psalms, are you pietistic? "Just pray and give it all to Jesus. . . . Claim back your inheritance from Satan. . . . Learn mindfulness and listen for the voice of God in your inner silence."

Unlike Jesus, do you speak in theological abstractions and generalities? "The sovereignty of God. . . . Justification by faith. . . . The synergy of God's initiative and man's response in the sanctification process . . ."

Unlike Paul—no two letters and no two sermons ever the same!—do you offer the predictable boilerplate of pat answers and pet truths?

Do you talk too much about yourself—or too little? Does your counsel sound like a self-help book? There are innumerable ways to run off the rails. But even if your counseling is ineffectual, off-putting, or harmful, you are still a counselor.

If you are a good counselor, then you're learning how to sustain with a word the one who is weary (Isa. 50:4). This is wonderful, nothing less than your Redeemer's skillful love expressed in and through you. You've learned to speak truth in love, conversing in honest, nutritious, constructive, timely, grace-giving ways (Eph. 4:15, 25, 29). You deal gently with the ignorant and wayward because you know you are more like them than different (Heb. 5:2–3). You don't only do what comes naturally but have gained the flexibility to be patient with all, to help the weak, to comfort the fainthearted, to admonish the unruly (1 Thess. 5:14). You bring back those who wander (James 5:19–20), just as God brings you back time and again. You're engaged in meeting the most fundamental human need, both giving and receiving encouragement every day (Heb. 3:13). In becoming a better counselor, you are growing into the likeness of Jesus Christ.

Pastor, you are a counselor—and much more than a counselor. A pastor also teaches, equips, supervises, and counsels other counselors. Is your preaching worth the time you put into it and the time others spend listening? The proof lies in whether they are growing up into wise mutual counselors. That is the call and challenge of Ephesians 3:14–5:2. Hands-on pastoral counseling never means that you become the only counselor in the body of Christ. You are training Christ's people how to walk in the image of the "Wonderful Counselor" (Isa. 9:6). This is a refreshing vision for the care and cure of souls! It is a distinctively Christian vision.

This small volume focuses on the counseling aspect of a pastor's calling. But other readers are most welcome to listen in. All human beings are counselors, whether wise, foolish, or mixed. *All* Christians are meant to become wiser counselors. God intends that *every* word you ever say to anyone is actively constructive in content, intention, tone, and appropriateness (Eph. 4:29). Those who face *any* affliction should find you a source of tangible comfort (2 Cor. 1:4). Wisdom sets the bar high. We are to become a community in which substantial conversations predominate. You who are not pastors will grow in wisdom by considering how pastoral work particularizes the wisdom of Christ in the cure of souls wherever the body of Christ is working well.

This volume has two chapters. First, we will discuss how to understand the word *counseling* within a pastoral frame of reference. Second, we will unpack a few of the distinctives that make a pastor's counseling so unique.

1

What Is Counseling?

THE PSYCHOTHERAPEUTIC CONCEPTION of counseling operates in a different universe from the pastoral conception. The human problems are the same, of course: broken, confused, distressed, distressing people who need help. How should we define the "talking cure" for the ills that beset us?

A therapist's treatment typically means a private relationship confined to an appointed hour once a week. Like medicine or law, the mental health professions treat patients/clients on a fee-for-service basis. State licensure recognizes education and experience that presumably grant esoteric explanatory insight and exceptional interventive skills. Like medical professionals, mental health professionals present themselves as possessing objective scientific knowledge and offering value-neutral technical expertise. The ostensibly healthy treat the definedly sick. A client's difficulties and distress are susceptible to diagnosis in morally neutral categories: a DSM syndrome, dysfunction, or disorder.[1]

Therapeutic professionalism serves a distinct ethos. Clinical detachment intentionally avoids the mutuality of normal social existence: willing self-disclosure, "dual relationships" that live outside the office as well as inside, the candid give-and-take of story, opinion, persuasion, and mutual influence. Professional reserve dictates that "the therapist will not impose or otherwise induce his personal values on the patient. . . . The exploration and acquisition of more constructive and less neurotically determined values [is] conducted without ethical or moral pressure or suasions of any kind."[2] Psychotherapeutic faith roots in "the assumption that in every human being there is a core selfhood that if allowed free and unconflicted expression would provide the basis for creative, adaptive, and productive living."[3] Religion is recognized as a factor that might be individually compelling for some clients, either a comforting resource or an aspect of pathology. But "God" has no objective significance or necessary relevance either in explanation or treatment of dysfunctional emotions, behaviors, and thoughts.

This constellation of assumptions and expectations expresses the professional self-image of the talking-cure professions. It shapes our culture's implicit belief that "psychotherapy/counseling" is essentially analogous to medical doctoring. But this complex of meanings profoundly misshapes assumptions of what counseling really is and ideally ought to be. Counseling per se is not like medical doctoring. It is pastoring. It is discipling. If we want to use the physician analogy, counseling is the "bedside manner" part of doctoring, not the medical part. It expresses the influence human beings have on one another's thoughts, values, moods, expectancies, and choices. Counseling is not essentially a technical enterprise calling for technical expertise. It is a relational and pastoral enterprise engaging in care and cure of the soul. Both "psycho-therapy" and "psych-iatry" attempt pastoral work. They engage in "care and cure of the soul" as their etymologies accurately signify. Sigmund Freud rightly defined therapists as "secular pastoral workers."[4]

Personal factors—who you are, how you treat people, what you believe—are decisive in pastoral work. The key ingredients in pastoring another human being are love, wisdom, humility, integrity, mercy, authority, clarity, truthspeaking, courage, candor, curiosity, hope, sane humanity, wide experience, much patience, careful listening, responsive immediacy, and willingness to live with uncertainty about process and outcome. Therapists also know this, deep down, and say as much when they doff the professional persona.[5] These are terrific personal qualities. They express nothing less than how the image of God lives in human flesh while going about the work of redeeming broken, confused, distressed, distressing people who need help. The mental health professions intuit well when they say that personal factors are the essential factors. But they serve in pastorates with no God and no church. They aim to restore straying, suffering, willful, dying human beings. But they consider Christ unnecessary to their pastoral work. As a matter of principle, they will not lead strugglers to the Savior of strays. You know better. But the secularized-medicalized definition of counseling powerfully intimidates pastors and laypersons alike. If the habits, instincts, outlook, and goals of therapeutic pastorates define counseling, then you had better not pretend or aspire to be a counselor. You need a different way—a better way—to understand counseling.

A Redefinition of Counseling

Consider four ways that you as a pastor must redefine counseling.

For starters, if the psychotherapeutic definition controls our vision, *what pastor could ever provide the necessary care and cure of even thirty souls, let alone one hundred, five hundred, or five thousand souls? What pastor has time to get the presumably necessary secularized education?* Having labored long toward your ordination by the church, who has time or inclination to labor for a second ordination by the mental health system? What pastor could ever invest so much time in one-to-one counseling? A pastor needs a very different vision for what counseling is and can be.

Second, *what true pastor believes that the love of Christ and the will of God are value free?* You will never say to anyone (except ironically), "You are free to discover your own values, whatever works for you, whatever way of living with yourself and others brings you a sense of personal satisfaction." God has chosen to impose his values on the entire universe. First Timothy 1:5 bluntly asserts nonnegotiable goals: "love . . . from a pure heart and a good conscience and a sincere faith." God insists on the supreme worth and glory of who he is and what he has done. God insists that self-centered people learn love—not coping skills, not self-actualization, not meeting felt needs, not techniques of managing emotions or thought life, not fulfilling personal goals. God's morally charged categories heighten human responsibility. His willing mercy and sheer grace give the only real basis for true compassion and patience. He insists that we learn love by being loved, by learning Jesus: "In this is love . . . that he loved us and sent his Son to be the propitiation for our sins" (1 John 4:10). On the last day, every knee bows to God's "values."

The whole nature of ministry is to "impose" light into darkness, to induce sanity, to form Christ's life-nourishing values within us. Pastoral counseling openly brings "ethical or moral suasions" as expressions of genuine love that considers the actual welfare of others. The conscious intentions of Christless counselors are kindly, but they do not consider the true welfare and needs of actual human beings. A pastor has a systematically brighter vision for what counseling is all about.

Third, *what honest pastor would ever buy into the arm's-length professional reserve of the therapist?*[6] Ministry is self-disclosing by necessity and as a matter of principle. After all, we follow David, Jeremiah, Jesus, and Paul. Shouts of delight along with loud cries and groaning are part of the whole package. No real pastor can be clinically detached. The Paul who wrote 1 Thessalonians 2:7–12 is far too emotionally involved. Like Jesus, he cares too much to ever stand at arm's length from people and their troubles. If Jesus had entered into purely consultative, professional relationships, he'd have had to stop being a pastor. Pastoral self-disclosure is one part of wise love. It is not self-indulgent. It is neither impulsive venting nor exhibitionistic transparency nor a pontificating of private opinions. It includes proper reserve. But Christian openness is a different ball game from the ideal of dispassionate professionalism. Ministry expresses the honest emotional immediacy of team sports and contact sports. It is full-court basketball, not chess or poker.

How about you? Don't people know you in all sorts of other roles besides counselor?—proclaimer of words of life, friend at the dinner table, bedside visitor in the hospital, second-baseman on the softball team, mere man and leader who can't help but show how he faces financial pressure or handles interpersonal conflict, object of uproarious roasting at the church retreat, public speaker who tells a good story on himself, host and landlord to the struggler staying in your spare bedroom, husband of a woman who is well-known in her own right, father of kids in Sunday school, fellow sufferer who needs what he asks of God, fellow worshiper who candidly gives thanks for what he receives, fellow servant who yearns to love better than he does. You not only have a dual relationship with the people you counsel; you have multiple relationships. And that's as it should be. Christianity is a different counseling ethos.

Finally, *what good pastor could ever in good conscience adopt the ethos by which the ostensibly well presume to treat the evidently sick*? Aren't we all in this together, facing the same temptations, sorrows, and threats? Aren't we all prone to the same sinfulness? "Behavioral medicine" (as the health insurance companies label it) claims to cure a patient's character disorder, identity confusion, mood disorder, thought disorder, maladaptive behavior, relational dysfunction, and post-traumatic stress syndrome. Ministry addresses the same problems but humanizes the struggle. A dark disease deranges our character, identity, emotions, thoughts, behaviors, and relationships. A bright Savior sets about curing such souls. Endemic sinfulness deranges our reactions to both traumatic and everyday sufferings. Psalm 23 infuses a different way of suffering. Our derangement is fundamental, rooting in dedicated attentiveness to our own inner voice, the liar we find most persuasive (Prov. 16:2; 21:2). But our Pastor's voice heals us: "My sheep hear my voice" (John 10:27). Don't you have the same kinds of problems as those you minister to, and aren't our differences matters of degree, not kind? Aren't you part of the same ongoing healing? Real ministry engages the same personal and interpersonal problems that the psychotherapies address—but more deeply. It pursues hidden moral cancers that we all share, whether our symptoms are florid or mild. And any healing is our healing, one and all.

Jesus Our Counselor

Where does this pastoral ethos come from? Jesus himself was touched with the weaknesses, struggles, and temptations of those with whom he spoke and for whom he died. Jesus eschews clinical detachment. He chooses frank self-disclosure and the multi-relationships intrinsic to pastoral love. He was never value neutral. He used every form of loving suasion, right down to publicly dying for those he sought to persuade.

2

The Uniqueness of
Pastoral Counseling

WE HAVE SKETCHED A VISION for counseling as pastoral work. What does it look like? We will consider five unique aspects of the pastor as counselor. Your responsibility, opportunity, method, message, and context are each unique.

You Have a Unique *Responsibility* to Counsel

You must counsel. It's not optional. You can't say no as if it were simply a career choice, a matter of personal preference, or an absence of gifting. This does not mean that every pastor will have the same balance between public and private aspects of ministry. How much you'll "formally" counsel (i.e., meet with particular persons at agreed-on times) depends on many factors. Some pastors will do a great deal of hands-on cure of souls, some relatively little. But every pastor ought to dedicate some percentage of his ministry to the delicate art of intentional conversation as well as being continually on the lookout for the informal opportunities latent in every human interaction.[7]

A pastor's calling to counsel is significantly different from any of the other counseling professions. We'll consider several aspects of this uniqueness.

Your call to personal ministry is woven into all the Scriptures. Many passages express the significance of hands-on cure of souls. The classic texts include Acts 20:20; Galatians 6:1–2, 9–10; Ephesians 3:14–5:2; 1 Thessalonians; Hebrews 3:12–14; 4:12–5:8; 10:24–25; and scores of other "one an-othering" passages. In fact, every place that addresses the specific concerns of a named individual can be considered a counseling passage. A pastor's counseling responsibility is unique. What other counselor is called by God himself to both counsel and train others to counsel?! Briefly consider three passages.

First, Jesus said that the second great commandment is, "Love your neighbor as yourself" (see Matt. 22:35–40). Love engages your neighbor's specific personal needs and struggles. Love encompasses many things: attitudes of patience and kindness; actions that meet material needs and offer a help-ing hand. And love includes honest conversation about what matters. Interestingly, the original context for the command (Lev. 19:17–18) makes a personal counseling illustration and application:

> You shall not hate your brother in your heart, but you shall reason frankly with your neighbor, lest you incur sin because of him. You shall not take vengeance or bear a grudge against the sons of your own people, but you shall love your neighbor as yourself: I am the LORD.

God chooses to go after one of the most difficult of all matters: how will you love kith and kin in their shortcom-ings? Love of neighbor is illustrated by an example of candid, verbal problem solving, in contrast with the judgmentalism, avoidance, bitterness, and aggression that come so easily. You yourself act on this command by doing personal pastor-ing with your neighbors. And when those you counsel have problems with interpersonal conflict, you help them to learn constructive, verbal love. What a promise you have! "I am the LORD" (gracious, compassionate, slow to anger, abounding in steadfast love and faithfulness, forgiving . . . while honestly reckoning intransigence). Personal pastoring depends on this God and then lives out the very image of this God amid the exigencies of helping broken people. You live out what is inside those last parentheses. Exodus 34:6–7 displays the goodness and glory of God . . . and goodness and glory are communicable attributes, the image of Jesus forming in us.

Conversational love takes many other forms as well. You will ask, How are you really doing? Would you like to talk? How can I pray for you? Where are the pressure points? What are your joys and your sorrows? Any secret gardens? Conscious struggles? Delightful victories? How are you doing with God and with your nearest and dearest? What burdens are weighing on you? When you did/said _____, what were you after? How are you processing anxiety, anger, or escapism? How are you handling this wonderful achievement or blessing? In asking and answering such questions, we enter each other's lives. These are doors for grace, because these are the places Jesus meets people. As a pastor, your most obvious neighbors (beyond family) are the flock for which you have personal responsibility. "Love your neighbor as yourself" calls you to counsel.

Second, consider the book of Proverbs as a whole. It's not wrong to preach from Proverbs. Wisdom herself calls out in the streets, inviting all comers to listen (Prov. 8–9). But you had sure better *counsel* Proverbs. Verbal wisdom is highly esteemed, and most of what Proverbs commends reads as warmly personalized individual counsel: like a father, like a wife and mother, like a true friend, like a good king, like any wise person. Wisdom *is* a counseling gift. When it comes to distributing this most valuable, life-renewing gift, God's generosity is blind to differences of gender, ethnicity, age, wealth, status, or education. Surely he will not lavish the desirable gift of counseling skill only to everyone else in the body of Christ while leaving out pastors! You are called to become one of the wise men.

Finally, consider Paul's letters to Timothy, Titus, and Philemon. They are examples of personal counseling captured on paper for all time. Each is addressed to a named individual, discusses particular circumstances, considers specific strengths and weaknesses, and builds on the actual relationship between counselor and counseled. As counselor, Paul is tender, knowledgeable, self-disclosing, pointed, relevant, encouraging, and challenging. Can you legitimately preach on what amounts to a personal counseling text? Of course. But would you only preach on a personal pastoring text, and not also do personal pastoring? Pastor, these epistles call you to pastor.

You are called to do the impossible. It is curiously comforting to know that your calling is beyond your capability. This is another way that a pastor's call to counsel is unique. You can place no confidence in your gifts, experience, education, techniques, professional persona, credentials, maturity, or wisdom. You are called to do what God must do.

In 1 Timothy 4:6–16, Paul exhorts Timothy to immerse himself in revealed truth, in a life of faith, in active love, in the work of ministry, in serving Jesus Christ. He is to exercise, devote, practice, persist. He is to watch closely over himself and what he teaches. Why does Paul so carefully drive this home? The reason is astonishing: "By so doing you will save both yourself and your hearers" (4:16). Come again? You will *save* yourself and your hearers? It's so. Who is sufficient for such things? God alone saves from death, from sin, from tears, from weakness, from ourselves. Christ alone saves by grace, mercy, and patience at immediate personal cost (1 Tim. 1:14–16). The Spirit alone cures the soul of suicidal selfishness, making a person and a people alive to faith and love. Yet this great and good Physician willingly uses Timothy, a mere pastor, as a physician's assistant in the curing process. He also uses you.

It is hard to shepherd souls, to combat intricate moral evil, to help people walk through pain and anguish. Gregory the Great called it the "art of arts" in his great treatise on pastoral care.[8] He thought the task of guiding souls far more difficult than the tasks performed by a mere medical doctor.

Think about that. The body is relatively accessible. It is often explicable by cause-and-effect reasoning and treatable by medication or surgery. But the "more delicate art deals with what is unseen,"[9] the irrational madness in our hearts (Eccles. 9:3; Jer. 17:9). When you consider the challenge, how is it that most churchly counseling seems slapdash, pat answer, and quick fix? A good medical doctor spends a lifetime in acquiring case-wise acumen. A mature psychothcrapist pursues continuing education. Can a pastor be content with one-size-fits-all boilerplate? *Kyrie eleison.* People are not served when the Christian life is portrayed as if some easy answer will do—a pet doctrine, religious strategy, involvement in a program, spiritual experience—and *presto!*—case solved. Again, hear Gregory's words:

> One and the same exhortation is not suited to all, because they are not compassed by the same quality of character. . . . In exhorting individuals great exertion is required to be of service to each individual's particular needs.[10]

A pastor's work is the art of arts.

You are called to do something so simple that only a Christian can do it. Hearts may be unsearchable and insane, but the word of God reveals the thoughts and intentions of the heart (Heb. 4:12–13). My self-righteous reaction to criticism may be an unsearchable morass of iniquity, but I can learn to name it for what it is, to turn for needed mercies, to seek and find the God who humbles me. We can come to know ourselves truly (though never wholly). Similarly, though the purposes and intentions of another's heart are deep water, a man of understanding draws them out (Prov. 20:5). You can learn what you need to know. Though you have no privileged access into any soul, though every strategy or truth can be resisted, though you have no power to open blind eyes or to make deaf ears listen, God uses your ministry to cure souls. Human beings are idiosyncratic in *every* detail, yet there is no temptation that is not common to all; you can comfort others in *any* affliction with the comfort that you receive in your particular affliction (1 Cor. 10:13; 2 Cor. 1:4). Fundamental unities make us comprehensible enough to significantly help each other. These are things a mere Christian can do.

Dietrich Bonhoeffer was raised in a sophisticated, modern psychological culture, and his father was a psychiatrist. Like all educated Germans, Bonhoeffer thoroughly absorbed the psychological models and psychotherapeutic practices of the great twentieth-century psychiatrists. But he had this to say about the knowledge and wisdom that make the decisive difference:

The most experienced psychologist or observer of human nature knows infinitely less of the human heart than the simplest Christian who lives beneath the Cross of Jesus. The greatest psychological insight, ability and experience cannot grasp this one thing: what sin is. Worldly wisdom knows what distress and weakness and failure are, but it does not know the godlessness of man. And so it does not know that man is destroyed only by his sin and can be healed only by forgiveness. Only the Christian knows this. In the presence of a psychiatrist I can only be a sick man; in the presence of a Christian brother I can dare to be a sinner. The psychiatrist must first search my heart and yet he never plumbs its ultimate depth. The Christian brother knows when I come to him: here is a sinner like myself, a godless man who wants to confess and yearns for God's forgiveness. The psychiatrist views me as if there were no God. The brother views me as I am before the judging and merciful God in the Cross of Jesus Christ.[11]

You might want to read that again, slowly—I speak as someone prone to skim block quotes. As a Christian brother to those you counsel, you know depths that other counselors cannot and will not see. You can go where they never go. You can bring the Savior of the world.

Where ministry is strong, pastors practice in private what they preach in public. Your calling uniquely combines public and private ministry. The Christian message preaches well to crowds. The Christian message converses well with individuals. Preaching and counseling stand in a complementary relationship, and no other kind of counselor does both. A pastor's working vocabulary and intentional activity must "counsel the word" as well as "preach the word."

Of course, up-front proclamation and in-private conversation bring the message home in very different ways. A talk is relatively planned, scripted, and structured. It usually involves one-way communication—though Jesus did have a way of flexing his message after an outburst from the crowd or launching a message based on a question someone was asking! In a sermon, you usually have a rough idea what you'll say next and where you'll end up. But giving a talk is different from the give-and-take of just talking. Conversations are extemporaneous, improvised, unpredictable, back and forth, messy—even when you come with a game plan. You never know what a person will say next. And since what you say is usually a response, you almost never know what you'll say in return. It's a bad sign when either party reverts to boilerplate, delivering a set piece or shtick. Counseling usually starts with immediate, troubling experience, and moves toward the God whose person, words, and actions bring light. In contrast, preaching usually moves from Bible exposition toward life application. The two aspects of ministry demand different, but complementary, skill sets. The Lord and his prophets and apostles move freely in both directions. Pastors need the complete skill set.

The church has a long tradition of well-reasoned practical theology and skillful pastoral care. Like any legacy of art and wisdom, without continual use and updating, ideas become cobwebbed, applications get out of date, and skills are forgotten. Several factors internal to the church blind our eyes to the pointed counseling implications of Christian faith. Among those who take Scripture seriously, ecclesiastical habits focus almost exclusively on the pastor as public proclaimer, team leader, and administrator. Skill in cure of individual souls is optional—and sometimes is even discouraged as a waste of time. These assumptions structure seminary education, ordination requirements, job descriptions, role models, and the priorities of actual church practice. They shape the illustrations used in books about ministry, the relative dearth of books on how to counsel biblically, and the common associations to "ministry of the word" that treat the phrase as synonymous with "the pulpit."

In your preparation and testing to become a pastor, perhaps no one ever said that firsthand understanding of people and firsthand skill in counseling are essential aspects of your pastoral calling. But it must be said and taken to heart.

You already are a counselor—all the time. A pastor is unavoidably a public person. Other people are always reading you, taking cues from you, sizing you up. Unlike other counselors, in an essential way your work life is not spent out of sight in an office behind a closed door. Whether in casual interaction, a called meeting, or public worship, your attitudes, core values, and functional beliefs are continually on display. Other people listen, learn, watch, and decide whether to tune you in or tune you out. The fact that you are not hidden is a unique aspect of your pastoral calling.

People know how you treat people. They know (or have an inkling) if you are honest (or dishonest). They know if you are kind (or indifferent, even unkind). They know if you are wise (or foolish). They know how you handle (or mishandle) the pressures of life. They know if you are humble (or proud). They know if you care (or couldn't care less). They know if you want their welfare in God's kingdom (or if you are building a kingdom for your ego). They know (or have a pretty good idea) if you are a good counselor (or a busybody, a pontificator, a slacker, a pat-answer man). They know if you are the real deal (or a religious role player). Since you fall short, they intuit your flaws already. They have some inkling of how you handle your failings and how you'll handle theirs. Are you honest with yourself before God, a person who finds the grace and mercy of Jesus? They know (or have an inkling) because you are not a "professional counselor" isolated in an office and self-protected by "clinical detachment." You live, move, and have your being in public space. If you fail the test, they won't seek you out, and they'll be guarded when you seek them out. If you pass, your counseling will gain a power for good that is unimaginable to other counselors.

It is daunting to know that your sins miscounsel others. Richard Baxter famously observed, "I publish to my own flock the distempers of my own soul."[12] He warned of the danger that "you unsay with your lives what you say with your tongues."[13] But it is a corresponding delight to know that God uses your honest faith and love to publicly counsel others, so that both publicly and privately you might bring others under the sweet rule of his voice.

If you and the church don't do counseling, who will? It is unique to your calling that it *matters* whether or not people find help in the church. Psychotherapists want to make a living, but in principle, as a professional courtesy, they are just as happy to have a struggler go to anyone else for help, even if another practitioner operates with a very different counseling philosophy. But the church must not give over the care and cure of troubled souls to other voices. Those voices may be well-intended, but when they try to fix "with God" problems using a "without God" message, you have a problem with that. The fear of the Lord is the beginning of wisdom (Ps. 111:10; Prov. 9:10). Consciousness of God is the starting point, the system-aligning principle, the architectonic prerequisite for making good sense of life. When friends, family, coworkers, the mass media, self-help books, or psychotherapeutic professionals ignore reality, they inevitably miscounsel. In Jeremiah's metaphor, they heal wounds lightly, "saying 'Peace, peace,' when there is no peace" (Jer. 8:11). I will say it again. Pastors must not hand over care and cure of souls to other voices. Any number of people, paid and unpaid, are more than willing to do your work for you.

You Have Unique *Opportunities* to Counsel

Pastoral counseling is unlike any other form of counseling because of the many unusual opportunities a pastor has to engage lives. Here are seven unique facets of the pastoral life that open doors.

1. *You have opportunity to pursue people.* Jesus Christ goes looking for people. He takes the initiative in loving. Even when people seek him out with their sufferings and sins,

they are responding to what they've heard about who he is, what he says, how he cares, and what he can do. In a fundamental way, our Redeemer always makes the first move, and his entire modus operandi is active. The good shepherd goes after the one that is lost, until he finds it (Luke 15:4). Good shepherds do likewise, creating counseling opportunities. You can ask, "How are you really doing?" or, "How may I pray for you?" in any context. The person's answer, whether candid or evasive, can become an opportunity for a significant conversation. When you hear that someone is facing trouble or going through a hard patch, you can stop by to care.

In contrast, all other counseling models are passive, responding rather than initiating. Psychotherapists must wait until a troubled person seeks aid or a troublesome person is referred by a concerned third party. But a pastor pursues, and people respond in a unique way to being actively loved.

2. *You have opportunity in crucial life situations.* You have natural access into people's lives at decisive moments of transition, hardship, and joy. They invite you in. You have license to simply show up. The door is open to you whenever important events unfold:

- engagement and marriage
- injury, illness, and hospitalization

- dying, death, bereavement, and funeral
- birth of a baby
- move into a new neighborhood
- loss of a job or retirement
- betrayal, adultery, and divorce
- a child on drugs or in trouble with the law
- catastrophic victimization by house fire, crime, or storm

No other counselor has natural access at the most significant moments.

It so happens that these events are the major stressors on every stress scale. It also happens that the inner reality of a person becomes more obvious and more accessible in exactly such circumstances. Is he living for true hopes or false? Are her fears realistic or distorted? Are their joys and sorrows appropriate, inordinate, or oddly absent? What do these insecurities or angers reveal? Where is this confusion coming from? The heart lies open. Furthermore, it so happens that people become unusually open to seeking and receiving counsel at exactly such times.

Consider one example. God says, "Set your hope fully on the grace that will be brought to you at the revelation of Jesus Christ" (1 Pet. 1:13). Those are nice-sounding words, pleasant to repeat. But when the heat is on, previously covert false hopes show up in high-definition video and audio. You have a counseling moment, and life-changing reorientation can occur. The combination of high significance, strong feeling, and unusual openness means that you have privileged access into the God-sent circumstances when people can grow up in faith and love.

3. *You have opportunity with both the struggling and the strong.* Biblical ministry is not only for troubled or troublesome people. Pastoral care serves both weak and strong, able and disabled, talented and limited, successful and failing. The gospel speaks life-rearranging truth into every person's life, "comforting the disturbed and disturbing the comfortable." Those whose lives overflow need to learn gratitude, humility, generosity—and alertness to temptations of presumption, superiority, and pride. Those whose lives run on empty need to learn hope, courage, patience—and alertness to temptations of despair, grumbling, and covetousness. All of us need to learn what lasts and what counts, whatever our conditions of life. All of us need to learn to comfort others with the comfort we receive from God. The Vinedresser's pruning shears are in every life. As a pastor you understand that every person you meet today needs to awaken, to turn, to trust, to grow, and to love God and others. Everyone needs counseling every day (Heb. 3:12–14). Even God's thriving children

need counsel (and counseling training) in order to better help their struggling brethren who are straying, discouraged, or helpless (1 Thess. 5:14).

No other counseling role has a vision for everybody. Other counseling models define some class of human beings as needing help and others as essentially okay. Christian faith defines every human being as needing the cure of soul that is a pastor's unique calling.

4. *You have opportunity with both rich and poor.* A pastor has a huge advantage over other counselors in that the counseling relationship is founded on loving concern, not fee-for-service. Pastoral counseling is a gift to the needy. It is funded by free-will offerings of the people of God, whether or not they are counsel seekers. Broken and distressed people rightly wonder about professional counselors, "Do you *really* care? Are you *really* my friend?" The gift of ministry takes questions about divided or suspect motives off the table. The exchange of money for time, care, attention, and friendship always brings a high potential for warping a relationship.

In contrast, a pastor has great freedom to work. With people who have money, you are in the unusual position of not allowing them to buy the services they want. With people who lack money, you are in the unusual position of not excluding them from receiving the help they need. A pastor is uniquely able to incarnate God's freely given mercies and wisdom. Counseling is caring candor (Eph. 4:15). When no fee is involved, your care is less ambiguous and your candor less constrained.

It makes a great difference that you come free. When the tithes and offerings of many people underwrite how the church meets counseling needs, it creates the best of all possible "delivery systems" for care and cure.

5. *You have opportunity with people who already trust you.* What is the first issue in every counseling conversation? Though rarely verbalized, every person who sits down to talk with someone is always asking: "Why should I trust you? Are you giving me good reason to trust you? Do I trust you?" If the bottom-line answer is yes, then the conversation might head somewhere constructive. Basic trust leads to two further questions that also determine the success or failure of the conversation: "Can I be completely honest with you?" and then, "Will I listen to what you say to me?"

Of course, questions of trust, willing honesty, and willingness to listen are often worked out gradually. But it is a unique aspect of pastoral work that you will counsel people who have already decided to trust you. They come committed to being honest and willing to listen. This trust arises because you are a known quantity. Pre-answering these questions in the affirmative gives an incalculable boost to the efficacy and efficiency of your counseling. You don't need to spend months building trust. You can cut to the chase because counsel seekers cut to the chase.

The fact that you are known and trusted also means you'll be the first person that others seek out to talk over their problems. They will be honest about the most delicate things: grave sins, deep fears, heartbreak, disappointment, fragile aspirations, underlying confusion. Otherwise unspeakable matters find words where there is trust. After you have listened well to these most vulnerable utterances—quick to hear, careful to ponder, slow to speak—you also find that people listen to you if your words are kind, illuminating, and true. What comes to the light can become light.

Other counselors rarely enjoy this privilege, but you may find it is a regular occurrence.

6. *You have opportunity with people you already know.* Not only do others know and trust you; you know them. As a pastor this creates another unique opportunity. If you've made any kind of effort, you already know your people. You are continually getting to know them better. Such firsthand knowledge gives you an incalculable advantage over the office-bound professional counselor. You know people by name, personality, and life context. You've seen them in action. You

already have a sense for strengths and weaknesses, besetting sins and flourishing graces, good habits and bad. How does a man treat his family? Does this woman pitch in to help? Is this a man who keeps his word, or have you learned to wait and see what he does? What is her reaction when she faces frustration, hardship, and conflict? How does he talk about the blessings he receives? How does she worship? You may know significant history and circumstances. You may know someone's family. You have natural access to many involved parties.

Wide-ranging knowledge helps protect you from some of the pitfalls that beset counselors. For example, counselors often hear only one side of any story. They are always vulnerable to spin and disinformation—facts and reactions may be true and plausible as far as they go but steadily mislead and prevent accurate, balanced assessment. Given various instincts of our fallen hearts, counselors are easily tempted to side with whomever they happen to be counseling (Prov. 18:17). When an aggrieved twenty-five-year-old paints her mother as a monster, is it so? Perhaps. But if you happen to know both mother and daughter, you may have more nuanced insight into what's going on. The fact that you may already know people and know them in context is a unique strength of the pastoral setting for counseling ministry.

No other counselor has a regular opportunity to get both a head start and a reality check on what you hear in private conversation.

7. *You have opportunity with people who already have a wise change agenda.* Not only do people know you, and you know them, but as a pastor you will counsel people who already have a pretty good idea of what's wrong and of where they need to grow. Such up-front acuity is never guaranteed, but when it happens, it gives your counseling another huge head start.

We mentioned earlier the basic questions of trust, willingness to be honest, and willingness to listen. The next watershed question in all counseling concerns agenda: "Why are we here? What are we aiming to accomplish?" In general, most counsel seekers come with defective goals:

- Change how I feel.
- Change my circumstances.
- Vindicate me.
- Give me a formula.

Counseling with any modicum of wisdom works patiently to change that agenda into "Help me to change." Christian faith and ministry fleshes out the change agenda in a particularly rich way:

Help me to change, both inwardly and outwardly. Let me see where I run astray. Let me grasp how Christ's grace and truth actually connect to my struggles. Help me learn how to turn to God, how to trust, how to love. Help me take refuge in the Lord. I need to set my hopes on what is indestructible rather than pursuing obsessive schemes for earthly joy. Help me see more clearly how I contribute to conflict and alienation. I need forgiveness. Help me to forgive and constructively love my enemies.

It's a counselor's dream whenever a person comes with such an agenda already more or less operative. If your church has any clear-thinking vitality, you'll sometimes—often?—counsel people who already have a feel for what's really at stake. Even having a roughly accurate agenda makes a big difference.

Good public ministry, robust small groups, meaningful friendships, and relevant private devotion form people who already know the framework of reality. They know the contours of the soul's struggles. They know something of how God connects. But all of us need help connecting the dots. We always need help overcoming the contradictions between what we know and how we live. Those you counsel need the wonderful surprises that always come when an honest seeker sits down for a patient, probing conversation with a wise pastor.

No other counselor gets regular opportunities to work with people who already have an inkling of what they most need. Like your responsibility to cure souls, your opportunities are unique. I hope this vision thrills you. I hope it nerves you for the long fight to bring pastoral achievement closer to pastoral aspiration.

The Way You Do Counseling Is Unique

From a distance, it looks like most counselors do the same things. They talk with people experiencing some sort of trouble. The conversation focuses on the concerns of the troubled party. Would-be helpers demonstrate kind and constructive intentions. They ask questions, elicit personal honesty, listen attentively. They give feedback intended to illuminate, challenge, give hope, reorient, affect, or redirect. Troubled people who take the conversation to heart and act on it experience some alteration of mood, thought, or action. But apparent similarities are like similarities between different religions. When you get up close, you realize profound, systematic differences.

Your counseling methods are unique. Your line of questioning moves in atypical directions. Your interpretation of the etiology/causality of problems takes the conversation to places no one else goes. Your self-disclosure and proper reserve obey a different set of principles, reveal a different set of purposes. You bear witness to the testimony of God himself, who made, sustains, judges, and saves. You act as physician's assistant, not the great physician. That affects a conversation in countless details of tone and content. The image you have of your calling as a counselor—pastor-shepherd, minister-servant, responsible brother, peer in the body of Christ, fellow sinner and sufferer needing a Savior—subtly and openly affects everything that happens.[14] This section could be book length, but I will highlight only one unique aspect of how you approach the art of arts: *You pray with and for those you counsel.*

Do you realize how unusual this is? Have you ever considered how significant it is that you pray as a matter of course, while other counselors don't pray? The designated psychotherapists in our culture—psychiatrists, clinical psychologists, social workers, licensed professional counselors, marriage and family therapists, etc.—in principle do not pray with and for people.[15] This lacuna in their practice signifies that they believe no outside help is needed, wanted, or available. They and those they counsel presumably possess everything they might need for making sense of problems and choosing to live fruitfully. The answers lie within the individual, combined with a supportive, insightful, and practical therapist, perhaps with a boost from psychoactive medication.

You as a pastor do not believe that an explanation and cure of human difficulties can leave out the active, intentional heart that is always loving either the true God or something else. Only an outside agent can turn a wandering heart into an attentive heart. A true cure of the soul can't ignore the active malice of the deceiver, enemy, and slave master of souls. In the fog of war, who will help you see clearly? Wisdom does not suppress knowledge of the living God. Who will deliver us from evil? When you and those you counsel lack wisdom, who will give what is needed? You need and want available help. Therefore, you pray with and for others. Teaching others to voice honest believing prayers is one prime counseling goal. You pray because people need forgiveness for their sins—you cannot grant that. They need a shepherd who will never leave them—you are not that person. They need the power that raised Jesus from the dead—so do you. They need the hope of the resurrection, that one day all tears will be wiped away and all sins washed away—you share the same necessity. They need faith working through love to become truer in their lives, to run deeper, to take hold of everything.

- You pray for people before you sit down to talk.
- You pray inwardly while you are talking.
- You pray with people as an appropriate aspect of the conversation.
- You pray for people after you say goodbye.

Your way of counseling is unique.

You Counsel a Unique Message

The uniqueness of your message is easy to see. But you already know this. I won't rehearse the unsearchable riches of Christ, or the ten thousand pertinent implications. But I do want to note the uniqueness of your message by contrast.

Every counselor brings a "message": an interpretation of problems, a theory that weighs causalities and context, a proposal for cure, a goal that defines thriving humanness. How does your message compare with their messages? Simply consider what our culture's other counselors do *not* say:

- They never mention the God who has a name: Yahweh, Father, Jesus, Spirit, Almighty, Savior, Comforter.
- They never mention that God searches every heart, that every human being will bow to give final account for each thought, word, deed, choice, emotion, belief, and attitude.

- They never mention sinfulness and sin, that humankind obsessively and compulsively transgresses against God.
- They never mention that suffering is meaningful within God's purposes of mercy and judgment.
- They never mention Jesus Christ. He is a standing insult to self-esteem and self-confidence, to self-reliance, to self-salvation schemes, to self-righteousness, to believing in oneself.
- They never mention that God really does forgive sins.
- They never mention that the Lord is our refuge, that it is possible to walk through the valley of the shadow of death and fear no evil.
- They never mention that biological factors and personal history experiences exist within the providence and purposes of the living God, that nature and nurture locate moral responsibility but do not trump responsible intentionality.
- They never mention our propensity to return evil for evil, how hardships tempt us to grumbling, anxiety, despair, bitterness, inferiority, and escapism.
- They never mention our propensity to return evil for good, how felicities tempt us to self-trust, ingratitude, self-confidence, entitlement, presumption, superiority, and greed.
- They never mention that human beings are meant to become conscious worshipers, bowing down in a deep sense

of personal need, lifting up hands to receive the gifts of the body and blood of Christ, lifting voices in heartfelt song.

- They never mention that human beings are meant to live missionally, using God-given gifts to further God's kingdom and glory.
- They never mention that the power to change does not lie within us.

In other words, they always counsel true to their core convictions.

As a pastor, you mention all these things, or you are no pastor. Even more, you are never content merely to mention or list such realities, as if a troubled person simply needed the bare bones of didactic instruction. Like a skilled musician, you develop a trained ear. In every detail of every person's story, you learn to hear the music of these unmentioned realities. You help others hear what is actually playing. A relevant, honest pastoral conversation teaches another person how to listen and then how to join the song. Need I say more? No one else is listening to what you hear. No one else is saying what you have to say. No one else is singing what you believe. No one else is giving to others what you have been given that you might freely give. Every person who "needs counseling" actually needs your unique message.

You Counsel in a Unique Community Context

As a pastor, you counsel within the church. That doesn't just mean that your office is located in a different building from other counseling offices. Your setting contains unique potentials. God intends that churches serve as schools of counseling wisdom. You serve a congregation of potential members of the pastoral care team. Furthermore, every person whom you successfully counsel becomes in some way a better counselor of others. I've witnessed this development hundreds of times.

Other kinds of counselors operate as private professionals in an office or as members of a treatment team in a quasi-medical institution. But therapists sometimes dream that counseling services might become truly community based. For example, Sigmund Freud dreamt that psychoanalytically trained community workers would fan out into every community to offer their services.[16] Over the past century many thoughtful psychiatrists and psychotherapists have candidly recognized the limitations of office-based professional practice and have longed for community-based "mental health services." It makes all the sense in the world, given that people's problems play out in the home, in the workplace, and on the street amid the relationships, exigencies, and contingencies of daily life. But secular counselors have been almost powerless to realize their dream of what is needed to get the job done.

You are living their dream.

You work within the ideal community context. The church's DNA includes wise counseling in daily life by people who already know and love each other. Troubled people find meaning and relationship in a natural social context, and people who find meaning and relationship are no longer troubled. The body of Christ is the ideal home for counseling practice.

I'm not denying that our churches fall short of this sweet dream—fall far short. When it comes to handling problems well and wisely, church can seem more like a coma, a sleepless night, or a nightmare. But our failures as the church always stand next to Ephesians 4. The dream will come true. Community-based counseling practice is in our eschatology as well as our DNA. Your task right now is simply to take the next step in the right direction.

I will close with a final perspective on your unique community setting. You stand in a tradition of pastoral care reaching back through centuries. Wise Christians have come before you. Set out to learn from your brethren.

Every pastor will profit by reading Gregory the Great's *Pastoral Care*, written almost fifteen hundred years ago. We may have better hermeneutics, wider doctrinal understanding, and more awareness of the richness of the gospel of Jesus. But Gregory has more awareness of the gospel's personal application, more case wisdom, more flexibility in adapting to human differences, more sense of pastoral responsibility, more humility about his achievements, and more alertness to the subtlety of sin. Stand on his shoulders.

Every pastor will profit from reading Richard Baxter's *The Reformed Pastor*. Baxter is dense, and, like all old books, dated. You won't do ministry in the same way he did. But if you sit with Baxter, you will become a wiser pastor. Similarly, every pastor will profit from reading Thomas Oden's *Pastoral Counsel* and Dietrich Bonhoeffer's *Life Together*.[17] Oden's digest of ancient wisdom will introduce you to wise pastors you never knew existed. Your church history class likely explored the development of doctrine and events in church politics. Oden explores how pastors pastored. Bonhoeffer's twentieth-century wisdom and example will inform and nerve you as you take up your unique counseling calling. Every pastor would also profit from carefully pondering Alan Paton's *Cry, the Beloved Country* and Marilynne Robinson's *Gilead*.[18] Why fiction? In both books, the protagonist is a pastor, and you will learn how Christian life and ministry work on the inside amidst the untidy details of life lived.

Of course, I think that every pastor profits by reading and hearing teachers in the contemporary resurgence of biblical counseling. Ministry never simply recovers wise nuggets from the past. Pastoral theology undertakes fresh work. Current writers address questions and problems the church has never before addressed, or has never addressed in quite such a fine-grained way. Not all of it will stand the tests of time, ministry, and Scripture. You will become part of the winnowing of wheat from chaff.

John Piper writes eloquently of how your life and your counseling must express the faith you preach. He shows how you must involve the body of Christ in this calling to counsel, because perseverance in faith is, always has been, and always will be a community project:

> According to Hebrews, perseverance of the saints is a community project, therefore we need biblical counseling as the lifeblood of church life. . . . Perseverance is a community project. I say it again, because this is the reason counseling *must* be in the church.[19]

Oh, pastor, your responsibility, your opportunities, your methods, your message, and your context are unique because perseverance of faith in Christ is, always has been, and always will be a community project.

Appendix

AS DISCUSSED IN THE FOREWORD, David Powlison worked for CCEF for several decades. The mission of CCEF is to restore Christ to counseling and counseling to the church. Over fifty years of ministry, we have developed a model of biblical counseling that aims to assist pastors and other Christian counselors to bring the word of God to bear on the problems of daily living (for more information, see https://www.ccef.org/about/ for more information).

What follows here is a wide range of resources that we hope you will find helpful to your ministry. It includes a few books that are both unexpected and broad ranging. David spoke of these often, because they helped him develop a fuller vision for humanity. Others are included in the hope that they might sharpen and enrich your pastoral care.

—CCEF faculty

Books and Articles by David Powlison

David would not have mentioned his own books, but they are certainly worthy of your attention. He sometimes referred to himself as an essayist, and the description was apt. Most of his writing is short, dense, purposeful, and always worth a slow read.

God's Grace in Your Suffering (2018) has blessed many people seeking hope and biblical teaching about their suffering.

Good and Angry: Redeeming Anger, Irritation, Complaining, and Bitterness (2016) is a penetrating look at how our anger does—or doesn't—reflect God's anger.

How Does Sanctification Work? (2017) is a short book that brings clarity to the process of change and growth. It condenses decades of teaching from his popular class Dynamics of Biblical Change.

Making All Things New: Restoring Joy to the Sexually Broken (2017) is a single-topic book offering insight and help for sexual brokenness.

Safe and Sound: Standing Firm in Spiritual Battles (2019) was his last and most personal book. It is a reworking and expansion of his previous writings about spiritual warfare.

In addition, David was the senior editor of CCEF's *Journal of Biblical Counseling* for twenty-seven years. During his tenure, he wrote over one hundred articles, some of which were later turned into books.

Books Recommended by David Powlison

In *The Pastor as Counselor*, you may have noticed David's affinity for literature. The classics listed below illustrate love, hate, death, broken relationships, loyalty, and change. These books share a complex view of the human heart and its moral conflicts and show that human beings cannot easily be reduced to simplistic categories. This was an important truth to David.

Conrad, Joseph. *Heart of Darkness* (1899)

Dostoevsky, Fyodor. *Brothers Karamazov* (1880)

———. *Crime and Punishment* (1866)

———. *The Possessed* (1872)

Gipson, Fred. *Old Yeller* (1956)

Helprin, Mark. *A Soldier of the Great War* (1991)

Llewellyn, Richard. *How Green Was My Valley* (1939)

Paton, Alan. *Cry, the Beloved Country* (1948)

Robinson, Marilynne. *Gilead* (2004)

Solzhenitsyn, Aleksandr. *The Gulag Archipelago: An Experiment in Literary Investigation* (1958–1968)

Tolkien, J. R. R. *Lord of the Rings* (1937–1949)

Wiesel, Elie. *Night* (1960)

Novels bring us into the heart of humanity. Biographies do the same. David's reading list included a steady stream of biographies of notable men and women. A related genre is first-person accounts of personal and psychiatric troubles. These provide helpful insights and evoke compassion for people who struggle with problems that are hard to understand.

Crimmins, Cathy. *Where Is the Mango Princess?: A Journey Back from Brain Injury* (2000)

Denhollander, Rachel. *What Is a Girl Worth?: My Story of Breaking the Silence and Exposing the Truth about Larry Nassar and USA Gymnastics* (2019)

Jamison, Kay Redfield. *An Unquiet Mind: A Memoir of Moods and Madness* (1995)

Reiland, Rachel. *Get Me Out of Here: My Recovery from Borderline Personality Disorder* (2004)

Sheff, David. *Beautiful Boy: A Father's Journey through His Son's Addiction* (2009)

Other Helpful Resources

This section provides information on additional resources that you might find helpful to your pastoral care ministry. Those written by CCEF faculty, including minibooks, are available through our website (ccef.org).

CCEF Minibooks

What CCEF staff hears most often from pastors is this: Will you please write more minibooks? You can find them on bookracks in churches, and they go quickly. Each booklet looks at a common struggle, describes it, and gives biblical hope and direction. They are useful for pastoral continuing education, sermon preparation, and distributing to your congregation.

These minibooks are written by a variety of authors including David, the counselors and faculty at CCEF, and a growing number of other pastoral counselors. Minibooks cover a wide range of topics: marriage and singleness, parenting, sexuality, trauma and abuse, temptation and doubt, as well as depression, anger, anxiety, and overeating.

Books Written by CCEF Faculty

Here is a list of books on counseling and discipleship authored by CCEF faculty. They share the biblical distinctives of *The Pastor as Counselor*.

Emlet, Michael R. *Cross Talk: Where Life and Scripture Meet* (2009)

———. *Descriptions and Prescriptions: A Biblical Perspective on Psychiatric Diagnoses and Medications* (2017)

———. *Saints, Sufferers, and Sinners: Loving Others as God Loves Us* (2021)

Groves, J. Alasdair, and Winston T. Smith. *Untangling Emotions* (2019)

Lowe, Julie. *Building Bridges: Biblical Counseling Activities for Children and Teens* (2020)

———. *Child Proof: Parenting by Faith, Not Formula* (2018)

Smith, Winston T. *Marriage Matters: Extraordinary Change through Ordinary Moments* (2010)

Strickland, Darby A. *Is It Abuse?: A Biblical Guide to Identifying Domestic Abuse and Helping Victims* (2020)

Welch, Edward T. *Caring for One Another: 8 Ways to Cultivate Meaningful Relationships* (2018)

———. *The Counselor's Guide to the Brain and Its Disorders: Knowing the Difference between Disease and Sin* (1991)

———. *Created to Draw Near: Our Life as God's Royal Priests* (2020)

———. *Depression: Looking Up from the Stubborn Darkness* (2011)

———. *Running Scared: Fear, Worry, and the God of Rest* (2007)

———. *Shame Interrupted: How God Lifts the Pain of Worthlessness and Rejection* (2012)

———. *Side by Side: Walking with Others in Wisdom and Love* (2015)

————. *A Small Book about a Big Problem: Meditations on Anger, Patience, and Peace* (2017)

————. *A Small Book for the Anxious Heart: Meditations on Fear, Worry, and Trust* (2019)

————. *When People Are Big and God Is Small: Overcoming Peer Pressure, Codependency, and the Fear of Man* (1997)

Books Recommended by CCEF Faculty

A list of helpful books has no end. Here are a few that have shaped our thinking and practice.

Austen, Jane. *Pride and Prejudice* (1813)

Baxter, Richard. *The Reformed Pastor* (1656)

Bonhoeffer, Dietrich. *Life Together: The Classic Exploration of Christian Community* (1939)

Eswine, Zach. *The Imperfect Pastor: Discovering Joy in Our Limitations through a Daily Apprenticeship with Jesus* (2015)

Gregory the Great. *Pastoral Care* (c. 590)

Guthrie, Nancy. *What Grieving People Wish You Knew about What Really Helps (and What Really Hurts)* (2016)

Haddon, Mark. *The Curious Incident of the Dog in the Night-Time* (2003)

Holifield, E. Brooks. *A History of Pastoral Care in America: From Salvation to Self-Realization* (1983)

Kapic, Kelly M. *Embodied Hope: A Theological Meditation on Pain and Suffering* (2017)

Keller, Timothy. *Prayer: Experiencing Awe and Intimacy with God* (2016)

Keyes, Dick. *Beyond Identity* (2012)

Langberg, Diane. *Suffering and the Heart of God: How Trauma Destroys and Christ Restores* (2015)

Lewis, C. S. *The Great Divorce* (1945)

———. *The Screwtape Letters* (1942)

Lloyd-Jones, Sally. *The Jesus Storybook Bible: Every Story Whispers His Name* (2007)

Miller, Paul E. *A Praying Life: Connecting with God in a Distracting World* (2009)

———. *Love Walked among Us: Learning to Love Like Jesus* (2014)

Oden, Thomas C. *Pastoral Counsel*, vol. 3, Classical Pastoral Care (1987)

Poirier, Alfred J. *The Peacemaking Pastor: A Biblical Guide to Resolving Church Conflict* (2006)

Tripp, Paul David. *Dangerous Calling: Confronting the Unique Challenges of Pastoral Ministry* (2015)

———. *Marriage: Six Gospel Commitments Every Couple Needs to Make* (2021). Previously published as *What Did You Expect?: Redeeming the Realities of Marriage* (2010)

———. *Suffering: Gospel Hope When Life Doesn't Make Sense* (2018)

van der Kolk, Bessel. *The Body Keeps the Score: Brain, Mind, and Body in the Healing of Trauma* (2015)

Notes

1. Mental health professionals diagnose their clients using the *Diagnostic and Statistical Manual of Mental Disorders* (DSM), which is prepared by the American Psychiatric Association. Currently in its 5th edition, the DSM-5 was published in 2013.
2. W. W. Meissner, "The Psychotherapies: Individual, Family, and Group," in *The Harvard Guide to Psychiatry*, ed. Armand Nicholi (Cambridge, MA: Belknap Press, 1999), 418–19.
3. Meissner, "The Psychotherapies," 418.
4. Sigmund Freud, *The Question of Lay Analysis* (1926; repr., New York: Norton, 1969), 108.
5. Readers interested in doing some digging will appreciate Armand Nicholi, "The Therapist-Patient Relationship," in *Harvard Guide to Psychiatry*, 7–22. See also Peter Kramer, *Moments of Engagement* (New York: Norton, 1989), esp. 182–218; and Perry London's classic *The Modes and Morals of Psychotherapy* (New York: Holt, Rinehart & Winston, 1964).
6. Not all therapists buy into the reserve valued by psychodynamic psychotherapists. For example, a Virginia Satir or Albert Ellis,

a Fritz Perls or Steven Hayes, brings a dynamic and charismatic "presence" into the counseling moment, freely expressing opinions, emotions, reactions, assertions, and personal testimony. In their case, what gives them the right to so freely push their values and perspectives onto others? The more detached psychotherapists rightly see the danger of charlatanism endemic to the more intrusive psychotherapies. But the more intrusive counselors rightly see that values are "induced" in every form of counseling, and that a pretense of neutrality only makes that process covert. Only Christian faith embodies a principle by which values can be openly and continuously induced without either bullying or manipulation.

7. For discussion of how much time a pastor should give to counseling and the sorts of people to whom he should give himself, see "Pastoral Counseling," in David Powlison, *Speaking Truth in Love* (Greensboro, NC: New Growth Press, 2005), 127–32.

8. Gregory the Great, *Pastoral Care*, trans. Henry Davis (591; repr., New York: Newman Press, 1950), 1:1, 21.

9. Gregory the Great, *Pastoral Care*, 229.

10. Gregory the Great, *Pastoral Care*, 89, 226.

11. Dietrich Bonhoeffer, *Life Together and Prayerbook of the Bible*, vol. 5, Dietrich Bonhoeffer Works (Minneapolis: Fortress Press, 1996), 115.

12. Richard Baxter, *The Reformed Pastor* (1656; repr., Edinburgh: Banner of Truth, 1974), 1:1:2, 61.

13. Baxter, *Reformed Pastor*, 1:1:3, 63.

14. For a discussion of how the counselor's role is conceived both in Christian ministry and in secular psychotherapies, see my "Familial Counseling: The Paradigm for Counselor-Counselee Relationships in 1 Thessalonians 5," *Journal of Biblical Counseling* 25 (Winter 2007): 2–16.

15. The odd counselor, out of personal religious convictions, might walk out of step with the professional ethos and step out of role. But as a rule, there is no prayer.

16. Freud, *The Question of Lay Analysis*, 98–99.

17. Baxter, *The Reformed Pastor*; Thomas C. Oden, *Pastoral Counsel*, vol. 3 in Classical Pastoral Care (Grand Rapids, MI: Baker, 1987); Bonhoeffer, *Life Together*.

18. Alan Paton, *Cry, the Beloved Country* (1948; repr., New York: Scribner, 1987); Marilynne Robinson, *Gilead* (New York: Farrar, Straus, & Giroux, 2004).

19. John Piper, "God's Glory Is the Goal of Biblical Counseling," *Journal of Biblical Counseling* 20 (Winter 2002): 13, 17.

Scripture Index

ccef

Restoring Christ to Counseling and Counseling to the Church

COUNSELING
ccef.org/counseling

WRITING
ccef.org/resources

TEACHING
ccef.org/courses

EVENTS
ccef.org/events

"CCEF is all about giving hope and help with a 'heart.' If you want to learn how to effectively use God's Word in counseling, this is your resource!"

Joni Eareckson Tada, Founder and CEO, Joni and Friends International Disability Center

"The vision of the centrality of God, the sufficiency of Scripture, and the necessity of sweet spiritual communion with the crucified and living Christ–these impulses that lie behind the CCEF ministries make it easy to commend them to everyone who loves the Church."

John Piper, Founder, desiringGod.org; Chancellor, Bethlehem College & Seminary

Christian Counseling & Educational Foundation
ccef.org

Also Available from David Powlison

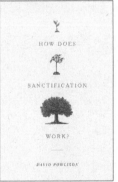

For more information, visit **crossway.org**.